THE TWELFTH OF NEVER

C·I·A·R·A·N

THE TWELFTH OF NEVER

C·A·R·S·O·N

WAKE FOREST

UNIVERSITY

PRESS

Wake Forest University Press.
This book is for sale only in North
America. Poems © Ciaran Carson.
Published in Ireland by the Gallery
Press, 1998.
First U.S. Edition published 1998.
All rights reserved. For permission
required to reprint or broadcast more
than several lines write to: Wake
Forest University Press, Post Office
Box 7333, Winston-Salem, NC 27109
ISBN 0-916390-84-5 (paperback)
ISBN 0-916390-85-3 (clothbound)
LC card number 98-61112

Contents

for Paula Meehan and Theo Dorgan

St Tib's Eve. *Never. A corruption of St Ubes. There is no such saint in the calendar as St Ubes, and therefore her eve falls on the 'Greek Kalends', neither before Christmas Day nor after it.*
— Brewer's Dictionary of Phrase and Fable

Tib's Eve

There is a green hill far away, without a city wall,
Where cows have longer horns than any that we know;
Where daylight hours behold a moon of indigo,
And fairy cobblers operate without an awl.

There, ghostly galleons plough the shady Woods of True,
And schools of fishes fly among the spars and shrouds;
Rivers run uphill to spill into the starry clouds,
And beds of strawberries grow in the ocean blue.

This is the land of the green rose and the lion lily,
Ruled by Zeno's eternal tortoises and hares,
Where everything is metaphor and simile:

Somnambulists, we stumble through this paradise
From time to time, like words repeated in our prayers,
Or storytellers who convince themselves that truths are lies.

The Poppy Battle

She wore the bit of the poppy between her teeth
Like a wound or a salve, while the ritual salt
Was spilled. The Civic Guards performed a somersault,
Then cleared their throats in salvo as she laid the wreath.

The former puppet languished in an unmarked grave.
I'd read about it in a powder magazine.
Light glittered on a detail of the architrave
In military hospitals that reeked of gangrene.

Red crepe fake felt paper poppy petals with their dot
Of laudanum in everybody's buttonhole
Exuded empty perfumes of Forget-me-not.

I dreamed they had inhabited the planet Mars
With shell-shocked, pockmarked soldiers on a long parole:
Poppy the emblem of Peace and the Opium Wars.

The Tobacco and Salt Museum

The Professor drove me into smoggy Tokyo
From the far-off airport in her unmarked Datsun car.
Acid rain hissed down. She wore a green kimono.
Coded neon glimmered in a game of rouge et noir.

You took a certain exit out of Shinjuku,
And found the Russian Bar the smallest in the world.
You filled the seven seats and stuck to them like glue,
And drank a measured amplitude of vodka, swirled

In momentary clarity. I smoked the Peace
You'd given me as broken token of the city.
Tobacco leaved and tumbled like a Golden Fleece,

I peered into a microscope to see the salt
In pyramids of Ptolemaic eternity,
Whereupon we stopped at this short, temporary halt.

Adelaide Halt

There is a smell of coal and iron. Black lumps
Of ballast gleam between the rained-on parallels.
I hear a blast of steam. Smoke floats across the dumps.
The platform trembles with the far-off decibels

Emitted by the almost imminent express.
Seventeen long coaches shimmered by to Dublin:
A blur of diners, drinkers, couples playing chess.
A sudden interim, then nitroglycerin

Booms from the quarry where they're mining basalt.
A gable wall says FUCK THE POPE. I feel exposed,
As fragile as a model galleon carved from salt.

Overhead, the adenoidal honking of wild geese.
Adelaide? The name? A city or a girl, who knows?
There is a drink called Hope, a cigarette called Peace.

Salt of the Earth

'Nodding buds with four crumpled petals, showy red,
Orange or white flowers, exuding milky juice' —
Was this the Soldier, Red-rag, Cusk, or Poppy-head?
The Sleepy-pap, or Fire-flout, Ceasefire or Truce?

STC gazed at the page illuminated
By a candle as he sprinkled his thesaurus
Over it to see the words hallucinated
Into sentences. He felt like Saul at Tarsus.

Whole fields in Flanders and Kent are salted with them.
Good farmers do not like to see them in the corn,
And call them cankers, whose growth they find difficult
    to stem.

Children's eyes are dazzled by these Thunder-flowers;
Crumpled Coleridge took an age to be re-born —
Poppy the emblem of Death and the Special Powers.

Nine Hostages

I cut my hand off at the wrist and threw it at the shore.
The goblin spilled a bag of red gold in my lap.
He wore emerald boots and a bloody fine cap.
Let Erin remember the days of yore.

I'd been riding the piebald mushroom for some time,
Following the Admiral's vermilion cruise.
He wore a blue cocked hat and tattered tartan trews.
We were both implicated in the crime of rhyme.

Up in the deep blue like a red balloon I flew,
Following the sickle grin of Old Man Moon.
Gun-metal gunships sailed in through the foggy dew.

In Creggan churchyard last night I fell into a dream
Confronted by a red dragoon, a green gossoon.
The red hand played the harp with oars of quinquereme.

The Rising of the Moon

As down by the glenside I met an old colleen,
She stung me with the gaze of her nettle-green eyes.
She urged me to go out and revolutionize
Hibernia, and not to fear the guillotine.

She spread the madder red skirts of her liberty
About my head so I was disembodied.
I fell among the People of No Property,
Who gave me bread and salt, and pipes of fragrant weed.

The pale moon was rising above the green mountain,
The red sun declining beneath the blue sea,
When I saw her again by yon clear crystal fountain,

Where poppies, not potatoes, grew in contraband.
She said, *You might have loved me for eternity.*
I kissed her grass-green lips, and shook her bloodless hand.

The Rising Sun

As I was driven into smoky Tokyo,
The yen declined again. It had been going down
All day against the buoyant Hibernian Pound.
Black rain descended like a harp arpeggio.

The Professor took me to a bonsai garden
To imbibe some thimblefuls of Japanese poteen.
We wandered through the forest of the books of Arden.
The number of their syllables was seventeen.

I met a maiden of Hiroshima who played
The hammer dulcimer like psychedelic rain.
The rising sun was hid behind a cloud of jade.

She sang to me of Fujiyama and of Zen,
Of yin and yang, and politics, and crack cocaine,
And Plato's caverns, which are measureless to men.

Fairground Music

I plunged my head into the laudanum-black pall
And gazed into the crystal lens of yesteryear:
A tang of Woodbine cigarettes and Phoenix beer,
Of bread and salt and cabbages, held me in thrall.

I knew it was a faery trick to take me from
The imminent republic of the future,
For the ballot-box contained a condom time-bomb,
And the red hand still remained without a suture.

I plunged my head into the lion's open jaws
And took the Ghost Train to Imperial Japan.
The tiny cabin smelt of alcohol and gauze.

Then everything was over in about a sec:
I glimpsed a skeleton or two, a Caliban;
I felt a damp hand fondle the nape of my neck.

Green Tea

I saw a magnified red dot on a white field.
I saw the terraces and pyramids of salt.
I saw a towering mushroom cloud of cobalt.
I made sure my papers had been signed and sealed.

The writing everywhere on walls illegible to me.
The faces in the crowds unrecognisable.
The labyrinth to which I hadn't got the key.
Investing in the Zen is inadvisable.

Zeno made a gesture with his disembodied hand.
A landscape wafted into being from his brush.
The flow of water is represented by sand.

If anything, I think I drank too much green tea.
The snows of Fujiyama had all turned to slush.
Hibernia beckoned from across the blue sea.

Sod of Death

'Tis well I remember the old Kerry dances
Under Astarte's ghostly light at the cross,
Where we'd jig each other's partners into trances
Fuelled by Japanese poteen and sticks of joss.

Then the Pooka would appear, to lead us o'er the moss
Into the realm of the Metamorphoses,
Whose shapes are as innumerable as Chaos
Ever burgeoning with versions of our species.

I was the wolf. She was the bear. I was the fly.
She was the salmon. I was the pig. She was the mud.
Then Cynthia herself joined in our revelry —

Her anorexic face, the craters of her eyes!
We saw that all Hibernia was drained of blood.
So we went with the flow, and entered Paradise.

Lir

Next to Poppy in the Herbal is Potato
Whose stalks and leaves and berries, like the Nightshades,
Are narcotic as the hemlock brewed by Plato;
Mashed-up, they make a pottage fit for renegades.

The tubers are not poisonous because they grow
Uninfluenced by light, which toxins seem to need.
Why, then, do I wander like a scarecrow
Blown by the autumn wind, like dandelion seed?

Our green fields have been sown with these Lion's Teeth,
Whose broken stems exude a bitter milky juice;
All Ireland has been turned into a blasted heath,

And coffins sail off daily for Amerikay,
As I do now, becoming this wild phantom goose,
Defeated by the wolfbane dawning into day.

Wolf Hill

Bring me my bow, my arrows tipped with aconite,
And I'll negotiate the border mountains high,
Protected by my sword and shield of samurai,
Which gleam beneath the wintry skies like selenite.

The moon shines like a globe of solid crystal salt,
A ghostly galleon ploughing through the tattered clouds;
I stalk the gloomy bog below which fog enshrouds,
And gird my loins that I might suffer no assault.

The haughty moon maintains her foreign silver coin,
And I have tracked the rough beast to his last retreat.
I slit him open from the gullet to the groin:

Therein lay little Erin, like one of the Undead,
A pair of bloody dancing shoes upon her feet,
Her gown a shamrock green, her cloak a poppy red.

Belladonna

I paid my passage with a coin of Spanish gold
And soared across the ocean to the promised shore,
Wherein I met a Caliban of ancient mould.
His eye was blue, his face was pocked like old Roquefort.

His running sores were patched with rags of Rebel grey,
His Phoenix talons bitten to their scaly quick;
He told me he had soldiered in the late affray
As double agent for the imminent republic.

Chameleon, he'd flitted back and forth between
Their shifting lines, being paid by some, by others not.
The pupil of his eye was bright with atropine;

He stared at me and asked, *O Death, where is thy sting?*
I answered, 'They have shot you with Forget-me-not,
And that is why you're neither man, nor beast, nor thing.'

Wallop the Spot

One morning in May as I carelessly did stray
Across the wild Slieve Gallon braes, I met with Captain Rock,
Who did salute me on the banks of sweet Lough Neagh.
He wore a wig, stilettos, and a poppy frock.

He opened up his Chinese box and offered me
A pinch of salt, some rare tobacco from his powder-horn.
Then he engaged me with the future history
Of Ireland free, where beauties waited to be born.

He wore a spot upon his cheek, an earring in his nose.
The pupil of his eye was black with laudanum.
The last I seen of him was hanging on a gallows

At a crossroads, with two other deviant brutes.
The next I heard of him, his skin was someone's drum,
His tibiae and humeri were Orange flutes.

The Lily Rally

The Papists stole me then and tried to make me play
Their Fenian music, but my loyal embouchure
Resisted them, and all the Melodies of Moore.
I threw their Roman legions into disarray.

My cardinal inquisitors were robed in red.
They touched their foxglove fingers to my breathless holes.
They murmured prayers for the saving of their souls.
They read their Riot Act at me from A to Z.

So then they built a bonefire for to burn me in,
Of broom, and brush, and willow, and potato flowers.
They bore me towards it on a purple palanquin.

As the flames roared around me, they heard a strange noise
Through all their chanting from their scarlet Book of Hours —
'Twas my ould self still whistlin' *The Protestant Boys.*

The Irish Exile Michael Hinds

Your air mail had a border like the Tricolor.
I slit it open with a knife of Damask steel,
As it exuded perfumes of a humidor
Replete with odorous tobacco and smoked eel.

Included was a Russian doll, a crystal rock
Of salt, a miniature of Japanese poteen,
A pack of cigarettes called Peace, a single sock,
A plan of ancient Tokyo, a sprig of green.

I took it I'd to meet you in the Vodka Bar
Beneath the rising moon of Gorgonzola cheese,
From whence you'd drive me in your toy Toyota car

Through intersections where the stop and go are garbled,
Where fluent crowds converge in milling Japanese,
In sequences of poppy, amber, emerald.

Wrap the Green Flag Round Me

At the Presidential ordination, Erin
Wore a silver wolfskin coat and gloves of kid.
Her bodyguard, a bearskin. All the knights were kilted,
The doublebreasted-suited dignatories foreign.

Above, the moon maintained her realm of a sixpence.
Dim bronze temple gongs resounded through the noon.
The courtiers performed a stately rigadoon,
While wheeling dealers made a ritual obeisance.

I felt the embouchure of trumpets in my bones,
The Sumo drumming palpable upon my skin,
The rattling of the chains below, and martyrs' groans.

I donned the magic mantle of the green gossoon
To spread myself into a fifth dimension.
I pocketed their Starry Plough, their pockmarked moon.

Dark Rosaleen

The songlines were proceeding at a daily pace
Like invisible barbed wire or whitethorn fences,
Running through the Monday of the market-place,
Where fellows mongered ballads under false pretences.

The port was packed with mountebanks and picketpocks,
Highwaymen on holiday, and soldiers on the spree.
Female sailors festered in the feisty docks,
And ragged rascals played the Game without a Referee.

I caught one by his buttonhole, and asked him plain
And proud, if ever dear old Ireland would be free,
Or would our forces be forever split in twain?

Could we expect the promised help from Papal Spain?
He caught my eye, and answered me quite candidly,
The only freedom that you'll find is in the dead domain.

The Wind that Shakes the Barley

Once down by the Liberties, I met with Captain Wilde,
Resplendent in a dogskin coat and rabbit stole.
He wore a green carnation in his buttonhole,
And looked the very image of a fairy child.

I took him in my arms and set him in the lap
Of my kimono, all the better for to see him,
And I kissed his bonsai hands, I felt his wooden limb.
Then I undid myself, and offered him my pap.

He peeped at me from underneath his bicorn hat,
And murmured, with the voice of a ventriloquist,
Just read my lips: the Eagle does not hunt the Gnat.

He bit the good side of my neck. I snapped at him
With quadrupedal scissors of the Tailor's Twist,
And made of him a disembodied interim.

The Tailor's Twist

It was clear the cluricaune had taken my bitch
Again last night for a ride, from her tattered pelt
And her poor ribs ranged in patches like a bacon flitch.
He did not reckon on the cunning of the Celt.

I stitched her back together with a spider's thread
And, with my foxglove thimble, gave her magic powers.
Next night, I laid out dribs of poteen, salt, and bread.
The cluricaune came for them in the early hours.

I watched him feed his face with food and salt and drink
Till, satisfied, he tried to jump my canine chum.
She twitched, and held him fast, and he began to shrink.

Then I put on my jacket of the hunting pink.
I penned his neck between my finger and my thumb,
And stuck the bastard's neb into a well of ink.

Catmint Tea

The cat and I are quite alike, these winter nights:
I consult thesauruses; he forages for mice.
He prowls the darkest corners, while I throw the dice
Of rhyme, and rummage through the OED's delights.

He's all ears and eyes and whiskery antennae
Bristling with the whispered broadcast of the stars,
And I have cruised the ocean of a thousand bars,
And trawled a thousand entries at the dawn of day.

I plucked another goose-quill from the living wing
And opened up my knife, while Cat unsheathed his claws.
Our wild imaginations started to take wing.

We rolled in serendipity upon the mat.
I forged a chapter of the Universal Laws.
Then he became the man, and I became the cat.

Spot the Wallop

The cluricaune, you must know, is a leprechaun
Who's taken to the drink. He also likes the pipe.
You'll never guess his proper name: he's called Anon.
You could mistake him for a naughty guttersnipe.

That's why the bottle of poteen you thought was still
Half-full is always empty in the blight of day.
And why do you think there's salt in the pepper-mill?
And why does the morning milk turn sour in your tay?

The cluricaune is wont to get completely pissed,
To stagger through your cat-flap like a cowboy shootist,
Of whose prankish misdemeanours I could make a list.

And it's ding, dong, bell, poor pussy's in the well,
The cluricaune is prinking in the dingly dell:
Scattered petals of the starlit Scarlet Pimpernel.

Let Erin Remember

Today we are celebrating President's Day.
Hence, the rows and the ructions at Lanigan's Ball
Are quite traditional. They dance an Irish Hay.
The gentlemen wear uniforms of tattersall.

The ladies favour emerald and cyanide,
A single glowing bead of amber at their throats.
They orchestrate their movements in a double stride,
One poppy shoe on show beneath their petticoats.

Each glitterata has a snuff-box in her garter,
Each dandiprat a twist of salt beneath his wig.
This night these will be strong media of barter,

When they lie down amongst the barley and the rye,
Beneath the moon, to play a round of thimblerig,
By which gambit they resuscitate the ambered fly.

Planxty Miss Dickinson

I've seen a narrow fellow tumbling through the rye —
You could mistake him for a whiskery ear
Of it, such is his camouflage of elfin gear;
And his whispery voice is like a mimicry.

Sometimes I see him casting a gossamer thread
To catch a butterfly and hitch a ride on it,
To waltz about above me like a drunken Zed,
Then vanish in a twinkling from my ambit.

And the drift of his speech is sometimes difficult to get,
Being wavery like blown grass, but I know some things
About its complicated phatic etiquette.

For instance, they've no way of saying yes, nor no,
For all their words and deeds are borne on viewless wings
Into the windblown ambiguity of snow.

The White Devil

I followed his vanishing footprints through the snow,
Beneath the moon, among the calligraphic trees.
Far-off silver temple bells were tinkling in the breeze.
Silhouetted on a branch was one black crow.

I offered it a pinch of salt to make it talk.
It told me of the wolfish fellow's habitat.
I tracked him to Slieve Gullion, just above Dundalk,
And called on him to make his requiescat.

He sprang a curse, and snarled his lupine length at me.
I sliced him four times with my sword of samurai,
And made of him a quadrupedal amputee.

Then I consoled him, saying, *All things have their span.*
He yawned his maw at me. Out flew a butterfly.
Dying, he became the head and torso of a man.

1798

I met her in the garden where the poppies grow,
Quite over-canopied with luscious woodbine,
And her cheeks were like roses, or blood dropped on snow;
Her pallid lips were red with Papal Spanish wine.

Lulled in these wild flowers, with dance and delight,
I took my opportunity, and grasped her hand.
She then disclosed the eyelids of her second sight,
And prophesied that I'd forsake my native land.

Before I could protest, she put her mouth to mine
And sucked the broken English from my Gaelic tongue.
She wound me in her briary arms of eglantine.

Two centuries have gone, yet she and I abide
Like emblems of a rebel song no longer sung,
Or snowy blossoms drifting down the mountainside.

1998

In this ceremony, the President will eat the host,
Which represents the transubstantiated moon.
Then Her Nibs'll christen the Montgolfier balloon:
Traditionally, it's always called *The Holy Ghost*.

She steps on board the gondola, and borne high
Above the madding crowd, she showers them with beads
Of mistletoe and amber, opium poppy seeds,
And little petalled parasols of madder dye.

Then all of us imbibe the haemoglobin wine
In dribbled sips of intravenous sacrament,
Where we combine in knowing what is yours is mine.

This is why we can commune so easily, I think:
Already, you've partaken of our President.
You ate her bread. You licked her salt. You drank her drink.

Drops of Brandy

I bumped into the fairy host last Hallowe'en.
I'd taken one or quite a few drinks for the road,
And so I thought I'd take the short-cut through Glenkeen.
A mist surrounded me. The light was blue as woad.

Then a disembodied hand lifted the thin veil
That separates us, and I saw their dancing throng
Of thousands, all arrayed in colours of the Gael,
Like figurines of jade. I did not stay too long,

Or maybe I abided a Gargantuan age;
But I remember being fed with cowslip cream,
And amber berries of a Lilliputian gauge

That shrank me to a blip in their crystal fishbowl.
Then they loomed through glass like Gullivers. It was no dream:
I swear to God, they left me home through the keyhole.

Mountain Dew

For everything can be contained in anything.
For every drop of rain that falls, there blows a flower.
For there are more then sixty seconds in an hour.
The long and short of it is like a piece of string.

For every line you write are countless thousands not.
For to travel is to go from where you've been.
For the first time that you read these words is sight unseen.
The knotted cord is implicated in the plot.

For fairies are not often seen without their nook.
For every hempen rope is wound of many strands.
For all the lies you told are entered in a book.

For dragons are implicit in the dragonfly.
The hourglass is complicit with its sifting sands.
For all the prophets claim, the end is never nigh.

Saké

The female puppet is legless. To make her walk
You must manipulate the hem of her garment.
Her hair is black as night, her face white as chalk.
Beware: she can turn suddenly violent.

When she is not active you must rest her on her stand.
Don't even think of throwing her down on the bed,
For you're the tool, and she the doppelganger hand.
To know her inner self will stand you in good stead.

Let the orbit of her eye accommodate you;
Put yourself between her poppy lips to make her speak;
Let her every practised action be your début.

For once I knew a character like you, my friend,
Who took his puppet drinking seven days a week.
A fortnight past, she took control. You know the end.

Who Ploughed the Lowlands Low

I know a headless corpse, a disembodied hand,
The mode of automatic writing on the wall,
A Cheshire cat, the Banshee's awful caterwaul,
The merrows and the mermaids basking by the strand.

One day, one became a mortal for a spell,
Entranced by a boy she saw fishing off a rock.
She followed him, abandoning her scaly frock,
Although to her the roads glowed like the flags of hell:

For every step she took she felt she walked on knives;
And everywhere her footstep fell, the poppies grew.
Her ears were tortured by the keening of fish-wives.

She haunted him for years within his rustic bound.
One day he went to sea. He fell into the blue.
She plunged in after him, and saving him, she drowned.

The Hag with the Money

It could be one of those lonesome bits of the road
Where water seems to run uphill, or a blue dell,
Or a pool where a prince might turn into a toad,
Where harebells grow in winter for an untold spell.

Or when you hear the weeping of a stolen child,
Or when the mountain shimmers like a purple cloud,
You hear the pourings of the waters and the wild,
Like chattering of fairies in a windswept crowd —

It's there you might well see a pair of cut-off feet
Come twinkling through the forest in their poppy shoes,
Unstoppable as driven rain or snow or sleet.

I know a woman was away for seven years.
When she returned, it seemed she'd little left to lose:
They'd drawn her teeth and danced the toes off her. They'd
    docked her ears.

Digitalis

Since I got my fingers stuck in a Witch's Glove
One night, my writing hasn't been the same, I fear;
And something's always whispering within my ear
About the murky underworld of goblin love.

That's when Mr Stump takes over — he who writes these lines
In automatic carabine — and I succumb
To all his left-hand fantasies of fife and drum,
Where soldiers sometimes use their guns as concubines.

Or often he describes a land across the sea,
Where all the men are uniformed in sailor blue —
His conversation's like the stumbling of a bee

Within a Fairy's Thimble — blushful Hippocrene —
And then he starts this cuckoo's rumour about you:
That's when I clamp him in my paper-guillotine.

Lord Gregory

There's muskets in the thatch, and pikestaffs in the hay,
And shot in butter barrels buried in the bog,
Extrapolated powder in the tin for tay;
And everything is wrapped in blue-as-gunsmoke fog.

It's that dewy blue of your mantle, Mavourneen,
Cobalt banner of the yet-to-be republic
Which enraptures us, as numerous as grass is green:
We are your unseen agents, growing thin and thick

In every patch of field, and briar, and the mireland.
Creeping through the thistled fields, we are the weed,
That disrespected emblem of old Ireland.

'Three persons grow from but one stalk,' so said St Pat,
'And you will propagate yourselves in thought and deed,
And what will you be then, O Peasant, O Aristocrat?'

The Blue Shamrock

Now they rehearse their ancient music on the harp,
And blow blue music from the bonsai bamboo flute,
The President is talking to the ancient carp
Which swims in green gloom in the Pisces Institute.

Like a ventriloquist she reads its silent lip,
Interpreting the gnomic bubbles of its word,
Which bloop like quavers of a psychedelic trip,
Or nimble foldings of the origami bird.

As a surface of the pool begins to ripple,
She undoes the couplets of her blue kimono,
And as King Fish comes up, she offers him her nipple.

This, Dear Sir, is when the spirit enters matter
Or, as a master summarized it long ago,
Old pond: a frog jumps in: the sound of water.

Sayers, or, Both Saw Wonders

We lay down in the Forest of Forget-me-not;
You slept, and from your open lips an Admiral
Emerged as if out for a daily ramble,
Quivering its wings as vivid as a Rorschach blot.

It crept down you, over a stream and through the rye
Into an open socket of an equine skull,
To wander for a lull within that Trojan hull,
Before it crawled out from the other empty eye.

Then it returned into your mouth the way it went.
You woke, and told me of your labyrinthine dream:
The highway — river — palace — rooms of vast extent —

'It looks as if the soul's a butterfly,' I said,
'Yet many who've elaborated on this theme
Have never seen the inside of a horse's head.'

Dancers

The Charlemont Arms was packed with twisters, quacks,
   and sailors,
Fawney-riggers, saltimbancos, jerks and twangmen,
Hog-rubbers, slobber-swingers, double-jointed men,
And knackered horses flogged by croppy tinker tailors.

Come night, they congregate to dance a langolee
Above the horse's skull below the flagstoned floor,
With nugging-dresses, quiffs, and other sorts of whore,
And pockmarked dandies wielding canes of ivory.

I met a Captain Cutter, as he styled himself,
As I went out again to plough the Rocks of Bawn.
He buttonholed my earlobe like a vampish elf,

And asked me would I ride the headless horse at dawn.
I shook him off, and hid myself within a stook
Of corn. He followed and took out his reaping-hook.

Clonmel Jail

My name is Captain Nicholas Hanley Caravat.
I'm famous throughout Ireland for my blunderbuss,
My brace of pistols, and my sword, for I'm a democrat:
These are my fellows of the agriculturus.

Who disregards us will be given warnings three:
The digging of a grave, the killing of a sheep,
The burning of a house. For all men are born free:
A naked fact that's feared by landlords, when they sleep.

Every dark or so, we'd come out in our women's clothes,
And work away until the crowing of the cock,
Till one of you betrayed me for an English rose.

And now they are about to hang me like a rat,
I blow a kiss, and throw to them my silken stock,
And help them fit me with their hempen caravat.

Milk of Paradise

I fell to drinking with a Doctor Tom de Quincey,
Who claimed he'd found the one and true catholicon
For palsy, gout, apoplexy, rabies, quinsy,
And every other ailment in the lexicon.

His compatriot, a Saxon rhymer of renown,
Had sipped this elixir to summon up the Muse,
Who blew him poetry like floating thistledown,
Spontaneous as the dandelion's milky ooze.

He drew an azure naggin from his shanavest,
And he exchanged it for my Irish two-pound note.
I downed it in three slugs of rhythmic anapaest,

And this is why you must beware my flashing eyes,
My floating hair, my pupils black as creosote,
With which I saw through Doctor Ecstasy's disguise.

Planxty Patrick Connors

The buttons of his vest were buds of opium,
The vest itself of tattered Oriental silk,
Embroidered with a riot of geranium
And emerald, and curlicues of Dragon's Milk.

Its pockets, fobs and slits were manifold capacious,
Holding in their depths the many sundry item:
Salt, tobacco, ballads, manifestos spacious,
Guns, pens, flint, steel, bone dice, coin ad infinitum.

His wounds were ponceau red, his face as white as milk.
He lay expiring on the kitchen floor, for we
Had tracked him to his lair, like others of his ilk.

He had a crossbow bolt embedded in each limb.
With claymores broad we made of him an amputee.
We decapitated him. Then we divested him.

Crack

This Fortnight Market last, I fell in with these Keogh boys,
Who plied me liberally with brandywine and snuff.
They showed me upstairs and took off my corduroys,
And dressed me in a raffish crinoline and ruff.

Next they walked me downstairs to their Captain's wake.
He lay trussed in his shanavest and caravat,
His sword and blunderbuss beside. He looked like William Blake.
Thirteen candles signified the sabbat.

The Locals then produced a rock of crystallite,
And short clay pipes, and crumbled leaves of Widow's Weed,
With which we chased the burning tiger through the night.

Come dawn, they asked me to fulfil my woman's role.
I breathed smoke into him, and said the Backwards Creed.
His eyes sprang open, and I saw his very soul.

Jarrow

I found him lying where they'd raked him with a harrow.
I kissed his wounds and thrust my bloodied lips to his
To breathe life into him, that we might see tomorrow.
I felt him pulsing as his *was* became an *is*.

I took him home and put him in my marriage bed,
And staunched him with a thousand leaves of Soldier's
    Woundwort,
And I bandaged him, and stitched him with a linen thread,
Then draped his body in my madder underskirt.

I left him dreaming for a month of Sundays, till
He woke one Easter, and unveiled his second life.
The iris of his eye was green as chlorophyll,

His pupil pansy-black. He glittered like a knife.
He spoke: 'Take me to that Saxon field tomorrow,
There to lie, and propagate our seeds of yarrow.'

Yellow

They made these four fields one, and planted it with rape,
Except the fairy thorn tree, which they left alone.
I'd often hide myself within its flowery cape
To contemplate the dreadful state of Ireland's Own.

A blackbird scraked a lyric with his yellow bill
From deep within the complicated maze of gorse;
I heard the wailing of a baby in a crib,
A passing tumbril drawn by the headless horse.

One morning I woke to find the mustard meadow
Had been mown into a burnished hieroglyph of gold
That spoke of harvest-bows, and lover's knots, and Easter
    snow.

I summoned up my ornaments of yesteryear:
Volatile rebel Easter lily, Orange bold:
Rotted buttonholes of triumph, peace, war, and fear.

Twelfth Day

Drunk as a bee that bumbles from deep in the bell
Of a Fairy's Thimble, in a heat-dazed summer meadow,
We sprawled as if we listened to a radio
Which broadcast nothing except insect decibel.

The volume of the field was many atmospheres
Of crawling, chittering, tiny Arcadians,
To whom teeming minutes might be days, and hours years.
In this vast universe, we were the aliens.

Every flower we saw, each stalk, was colonized
By troops of little fellows marching up and down
In perfect harmony, as if transistorized.

I went to pinch one 'twixt my index and my thumb,
When someone turned the volume up in Portadown,
And then I heard the whole field pulsing like an Orange drum.

The Ay O'Haitch

We march the road like regular quaternions
In jackets of the froggy green, and Paddy hats.
Our socks are gartered and our hair in Croppy plaits:
We are the Ancient Order of Hibernians.

Our silken banners waver in the dewy breeze
With emblematic gold embroidery of Ireland:
Wolfhound, Shamrock, Harp, the Plough in Hyades —
Five provinces not fingered by a severed hand.

We blow a fife tune on our red accordions,
And thrum the goatskins of our borrowed Lambeg drums,
For we're the Noble Order of Hibernians.

We are pedestrians, we're not equestrians;
We will outbreed the others; we have done our sums.
Will you, Sir, join our Union of Hibernians?

Centaur

Today the President reviews her regiments
Of troop and horse, resplendent in their uniform
Of Prussian blue. They are her true communicants.
Cherry blossom rains down on them like a snowstorm.

She reviews the veterans tomorrow fortnight,
Whose gorgeous tattered raiments are now badged with red;
And some have one eye; one stoops like a troglodyte;
And some with three eyes couldn't make it here; they're dead.

Some others share three legs, and some have none at all,
And most have digits missing, or a bit of brain;
As for the knackered steeds, their canter is a crawl.

She gazed into her globe memento of Japan,
And shook its bubble world of contraband cocaine.
Bonsai monster: horse's temple, torso of a man.

The Londonderry Air

Snow falls eternally within my souvenir
Of him, who wore the suit of Lincoln corduroy.
He was my noble pikeman, and my pioneer;
Snow falls eternally upon my Danny Boy.

I used to see him at the rising of the moon
With other fellows, exercising in the field,
For they'd refused to take the Saxon gold doubloon —
Indomitable hearts of steel, who'd never yield!

One Sunday, coming home from Mass, from him I stole
A kiss; he left on Monday for to join the war;
I never saw him more, yet he resides within my soul

Like some strange seedling of the plant of Liberty,
That breeds eternally beneath the Northern Star,
Returning as the blossom on the whitethorn tree.

No Tengo Mas Que Dar Te*

This salamander pendant is a dragoneen
Of ruby-studded, modelled gold, with pearls for eyes,
Which divers salvaged from the forty depths of green,
Where lay the wreckage of a former enterprise.

Survivor both of fire and water, noble gremlin,
Someone pinned you to a navigator's doublet
As an emblem to be borne through thick and thin,
So that their love might read forever like a couplet.

I think of her whose hand once held this wingèd thing,
Which I now clasp in mine; I feel an aftershock
As if our fingers touched; O Death, where is thy sting?

And now her sailor's long since made his final voyage,
He's been stripped of all appurtenants of wedlock,
Since they plucked the salamander from his rib-cage.

*I have nothing more to give thee.

Found

Agnus Dei reliquary, arquebuses,
Awls and astrolabes; beads, bellows, buckles, breech-blocks;
Candle holders, collars, cords and crucifixes;
Dagger hilts and dishes; ewers, esmerils and flintlocks.

Gaiters, goatskins, goblets, gunner's rules and glasses;
Heddles, holsters; ingots, jug-spouts, keys; a lion mask;
Mallets, Ming, muskets; nails; an oriflamme of damask;
Pearls, pellets; querns; ramrods, rings, and silver tasses.

Spokes, shoes, shot, steelyards, shackles; two escudo pieces;
Toggles, tweezers, tambourines and taper-sticks;
Urns and ukeleles; vices, yokes, axes, adzes —

Not to mention the admiral's medallion,
Nor the golden chalice, nor the Eucharistic pyx:
All these were found on board the foundered Spanish galleon.

Manifest

I saw the ghostly galleon late this Hallowe'en,
Its rigging cobweb-rimmed with filigree of salt,
Where wraithlike sailors flitted like so many shades of green
Within deep woods they sailed beneath the starry vault.

It seemed the vessel brought its stormy ambit with it,
Slow tornado crackling through the atmosphere
Of windswept branches amid sparks of moonlit violet,
Its steersman at the tiller like a gondolier.

A ladder was let down for me; I climbed on board.
Seized by disembodied hands, I was transported to
Their eerie captain. He unscabbarded his sword.

He asked me plain, what I had thought or done or said
To make Old Ireland free, or had I fought at Waterloo?
I had no answer for him. He chopped off my head.

The Horse's Mouth

I got that story from the Pooka, who appeared
To me last night. He stepped out from the wardrobe door,
Shimmering in its deteriorating mirror,
Shivering the fringes of his ectoplasmic beard.

I saw my breath as visible to him as nebulae
Of chalky sentences he'd drawn with a hook
From deep within me. Then he read me like a book.
I tried to speak, but there was nothing I could say.

I travelled through an hourglass of Saharan time
To universes unexplored by Star Trek,
Where monsters gyred and gimbled in primordial slime;

'And here,' he said, 'the worms devoured your eyes, and here,
The vultures scrabbed your heart, the vampires lanced your
    neck —
All this,' quoth he, 'to teach you necessary fear.'

Fear

I fear the vast dimensions of eternity.
I fear the gap between the platform and the train.
I fear the onset of a murderous campaign.
I fear the palpitations caused by too much tea.

I fear the drawn pistol of a rapparee.
I fear the books will not survive the acid rain.
I fear the ruler and the blackboard and the cane.
I fear the Jabberwock, whatever it might be.

I fear the bad decisions of a referee.
I fear the only recourse is to plead insane.
I fear the implications of a lawyer's fee.

I fear the gremlins that have colonized my brain.
I fear to read the small print of the guarantee.
And what else do I fear? Let me begin again.

Fuji Film

I feared the yen was starting to decline again,
Devaluing my take-home honorarium.
I joined the crowd that swarmed beneath the acid rain
Like schools of fishes in a vast aquarium.

Some wore sharkskin suits that shimmered like a rainbow;
Some were surgeons, with a white mask where their mouth
    should be;
Some bore barracuda grins, and some wore minnow;
One fat businessman swam like a manatee.

I saw two lobster samurai produce their swords
Of infinitely hammered folded Zeno steel,
That glittered like the icy blue of Northern fjords.

I snapped them slashing floating dollar bills in half
Beneath the signs for Coke, the giant neon roulette wheel,
The money index pulsing like a cardiograph.

Con Script

Had I all the money that I left in your store,
Hard-hearted landlady, I'd not bide here tonight,
But I'd ride on my horse in the silvery light,
And buy myself an élite military corps.

For I have had enough of drinking in the dawn,
And tinkering and labouring for beer and bed.
But I will be resplendent in my jacket red
As I parade my soldiers on the Royal lawn.

Her Majesty will draw me to her side, and ask
For my advice on how she might promote the war.
She'll offer me a sip of cordial from her hip-flask.

'Give me six Irishmen like me, and we will make
A constellation pointing at the Northern Star;
Our swords of light will ravage Ulster, for your sake.'

Picador

We swept through Austerlitz and Friedland like a plough
Through bloodied water, and all Europe cowered.
But when we came to Moscow, we were overpowered
By snow; our horses wallowed in the wintry slough.

Up to the stirrups in it, they plunged this way and that,
Slowly scattering across the moonlit landscape.
The Cossack dogs snapped at our heels. We'd no escape.
The huge stars glittered in their frozen concordat.

We found ourselves alone on the edge of a wood,
My horse and I, where wolves howled like a hundred banshees.
My bullets were all spent. I had no food.

I carved the horse's belly open and I crawled
Inside. I ate her flesh for weeks, expiring by degrees.
Some day you'll find us where her bones and mine are sprawled.

Mustard

Populated by poppies, these fields of '14.
The dreams of warriors blow through the summer grass.
Remember the dead by this pane of stained glass.
The bluebells represent their lips of cyanine.

The statues of the saints are draped at Passiontide.
Please take the transubstantiated wine and bread.
The drunken soldiery had taken to the bed.
You'll get a whiff of ethylene and sulphur chloride.

Then came the Angels, with their flaming swords of light.
Church bells doomed and gonged above the town of Mons.
The Tommies rallied, and the Huns were put to flight.

Do you want to try the demonstration gas-mask?
The campaign included many oxymorons.
You want to know how many yards we gained? Don't ask.

Banana Tree

The President is bringing many things to mind
By gazing at the cherry-blossom as it blooms:
Dead young samurai; the harvest moon; a drawn blind;
Stiletto tilt of footsteps in deserted rooms.

This road: no going-person on it; twilight falls:
The President is listening for the temple bell,
And as she hears the frog splash in the holy well,
June rain's still falling through the roofs of marble halls.

And now the cherry blossom's blown from the bough —
Snow that we two looked at, did it fall again this year? —
The President divests herself of here and now

And transubstantiates herself into a swan,
Which disappears into a higher atmosphere:
Full moon: a walk around the pond; the night is gone.

1795

Lodgings for the night! Threw down his sword. Snow
    swirled in.
We made the circle wider round the blazing fire,
And dared not say aloud, *Look what the wind blew in,*
For he was someone; we could tell by his attire.

He opened up his jacket of the Arden green
To show two pistols hanging from a bandoleer,
His gorgeous waistcoat fit for any queen,
All in the highest fashion of a Volunteer.

A year or three went by, but still we minded him
Who'd staggered in that night, and every word he spoke,
For rebel armies rose up in the interim.

And now I'm standing in Downpatrick Jail, I stare
At him they're going to dangle from their tree of oak,
And know him from his dying words, the Man-from-
    god-knows-where.

Spenser's Ireland

Rakehelly horseboys, kernes, gallowglasses, carrows,
Bards, captains, rapparees, their forward womenfolk,
Swords, dice, whiskey, chess, harps, word-hoards, bows
   and arrows:
All are hid within the foldings of their Irish cloak.

Fit house for an outlaw, meet bed for a rebel,
This whore's wardrobe is convenient for a thief;
And when it freezes, it becomes his tabernacle,
In whose snug he finds Hibernian relief.

Then there is this big thick bush of hair hanging down
Over their eyes — a *glib*, they call it in their spake;
They do not recognise the power of the Crown.

At the drop of a hat they are wont to vanish
Into deep dark woods. Forever on the make,
They drink and talk too much. Not all of it is gibberish.

Sunderland and Spencer

Here's Sunderland, resplendent in a foppish wig,
And Spencer in his doublebreasted overcoat:
You'll see them wheel round Phoenix in their horse and gig,
Reciting rather graphic Latin verse by rote.

Come glim of night, they flit to rakish gambling-clubs,
Or candle-lit bordellos, as the mood would take them,
Rooms in private houses that were fangled pubs —
That garter in the mirror, that uplifted hem!

Then both were smitten by the lovely Erin, who'd
Seduced them by her words of faery glamour,
And her eyes a double-glimmer 'neath her riding-hood.

There was nothing for it but a duel. Fencer
Stuck the other with his point of Latin grammar.
'I think,' said Sunderland, 'we can dispense with Spencer.'

The Display Case

Last night Hibernia appeared to me in regal frame,
In Creggan churchyard where I lay near dead from drink.
'Take down these words,' she said, 'that all might know
   my claim.'
I opened up a vein and drew my blood for ink —

I'd no accoutrements of writing, save the knife;
The pen she gave me was a feather from her plumage,
And my arm the parchment where I'd sign away my life.
'You seem,' she says, 'to have a problem with the language,

'Since you've abandoned it for lisping English,
Scribbling poems in it exclusively, or so I'm told.
Turncoat interpreter, you wonder why I languish?'

Her full speech is tattooed for all time on my mummied arm,
A relic some girl salvaged from the scaffold
Where they quartered me. *God keep the Irish from all harm!*

February Fourteen

Meanwhile, back in Japan, it is Valentine's Day.
The love hotels are fully booked as Bethlehem,
As, canted like a drunken boulevardier,
My soul roams Tokyo holding one rose by its stem.

Snow is falling in the print by Hiroshige
That I gaze at in a hundred TV screens;
Bronze temple-gongs reverberate their cloisonée;
The light is orange-syncopated reds and greens.

Then I met you, Irish exiles, in the Fish Bar,
Where we staggered between three wobbly shamrock stools
Eyed by prismed species pouting in their glazed bazaar.

Fourteen Bloody Marys later you lisped of home.
We then discovered we had come from different schools,
Yet thought the same, like mutants of one chromosome.

Hippocrene

Tomato juice, black pepper, Worcester sauce — a dash —
Tabasco, salt, the vodka measured to your taste.
Ice-cubes, ditto. Then sip this freezing balderdash;
Think about it. It is not to be consumed in haste.

Immediately ensanguined, your lips tremble and burn,
As if they'd got a massive intravenous shot
Of haemoglobin, and you're drinking from a Grecian urn;
The bar you understand you're in is called The Elfin Grot.

Karaoke singers mouth their lip-synch rhymes.
Tape-loop music tinkles harp arpeggios of ice.
The videos are showing scenes of ancient times:

Here is Moscow burning, horses led to slaughter,
Wandering the snowy waste of martial sacrifice,
Trails of blood emblazoned in the frozen water.

The Arterial Route

The sedge is withered from the lake, and no birds sing.
Above the dark pines, dim sun like a paper moon.
Leading his starved horse, a samurai's returning
From an ancient war. Cold, this early afternoon.

I noted his dented armour and his rusty sword,
His visage lily-white and scarred with starry eyes.
I then approached and boldly asked him for his word
About the last campaign, and was it truth or lies?

'I met a Lady once,' he said, 'a fairy's child.
I sat her on my steed. She showed me everything.
She fed me Milk of Paradise and honey wild.

'I saw pale warriors assembled in the Hall.
They kissed me with their starvèd lips. You feel the sting?
You cannot leave me now. You too are in her thrall.'

The Groves of Blarney

If you ever go across the sea to Ireland,
You'll find they speak a language that you do not know,
And all their time's a grand divertimento,
Dancing jigs and reels to McNamara's Band.

'Tis there you'll find the woods of shamrock and shillelagh.
And the pratie gardens full of Easter snow;
You'll hear the blackbird sing a gay risorgimento,
And see Venus rising at the dawning of the day.

Here they'll feed you hot mugs of buttered poteen,
Salty rashers, gander eggs, and soda bread,
And funny cutty pipes of blissful nicotine.

You'll find you will succumb to their endearing charms,
For sometimes they cohabit with the living dead,
And often wake in strange beds, and another's arms.

Finding the Ox

A Zen warrior searches for inner peace.
His bow is like a harp, that he might twang its string
In lonely combat with himself, and so release
The arrow of desire. An archer should want nothing.

His is the blue music of what is happening.
His sword rings true. Its many lives of hammered steel
Were there before him, and he trusts its weighty swing.
He knows the rallentando of a roulette wheel,

Or red leaves floating in a stream of eau de nil,
Bisected by a showy rival blade, while his
The leaves avoided. He's the opposite of zeal.

When he aims at the bull he closes his eyes.
Sometimes he hits it dead-on with a mighty whizz.
Sometimes he's way off target, which is no surprise.

Eau de Nil

That gorgeous warrior of Egypt, the Mameluke,
Habitually carries all his worldly goods about
His person like a most capacious pocketbook.
If not so burdened with gear he could swim like a trout.

Snuff-box, tobacco-pouch, salt-cellar, worry-beads,
Bouzouki, waterbottle, reliquaries, amulets,
Bejewelled scimitar, papyrus property deeds,
Three four-foot lances, fistfuls of pistols, bullets.

Come that July, he faced Napoleon Bonaparte
Beneath the pyramids of forty centuries.
He pranced about like he was Bony's counterpart.

Shot down or drowned in the Nile were the Mamelukes;
For a fortnight the French pillaged their laden bodies
With bayonets they'd beaten into fishing-hooks.

Trooping the Colours

Breeches, gaiters, busbies, turnbacks, epaulettes, and plumes;
Dolmans, girdles, cloaks of tiger-skin, valises;
Jackets, waistcoats, frocks, the fruit of many looms;
Bicorns, sashes, shakos, piping, braid, pelisses —

Carmine, pike-grey, crab-red, drab, philemot-yellow;
Yolk, parrot- popinjay- or rifle-green, and buff;
Garter-blue and amaranth, raspberry, tobacco;
Cornflower, chamois, madder, pompadour, and snuff —

So we paraded in our catwalk carapace.
Light flittered round us from our lances and swords.
A bugle call, a drum-roll, and off we marched to face

The enemy. Our motto was, *In God We Trust*.
See me now in my tattered petticoat and cords,
Blackened by powder and blood, and raddled with rust.

The Year of the French

Come nightfall, drugged with honied cakes of opium,
We'd hear the droning of innumerable bees,
The calls of owls and crocodiles within the cranium:
Visitations, some said, of Egyptian deities.

Hieroglyphic forms flitted between the low camp-fires,
Past dozing sentries, as if orchestrated by
The distant strumming of innumerable lyres;
To pass the time we would count the stars in the sky —

Galactic battalions of those fallen in war.
We'd hear the footsteps of their walking mummied dead
Retreating into the shifting interior.

Murmuring the names of our selves, that they might be known,
We'd carve them with our bayonets on a Pharaoh's head.
Let you trace them in a future black as the Rosetta stone.

Legions of the Dead

The key to Hieroglyphic and Demotic was the Greek —
Timeless rolling syllables of stout Achilles —
Indomitable body carved by Praxiteles —
Metamorphoses of martial words we speak.

My Irish is corrupted by the English tongue —
Emperor or Pharaoh in a Trojan horse —
Rape-and-pillage dragon-boats of Ancient Norse —
The now-forgotten lyrics of a rebel song —

The hand cut off and thrown to the Ulster shore —
The harp that once resounded in the High King's hall —
The indecipherable babble of days of yore.

Their armies were composed of hieroglyphic men
Like us, who marched through history, and saw kings fall.
Opposing soldiers are at one within our regimen.

Banners

For all that died from shot and sword, more died of disease:
Plagues, dysentery, miasmas, suppurating grot
Beyond the non-existent doctors' expertise.
Some were given military burials, others not.

Starved with cold, *La Grande Armée*, like dots in domino,
Stumbled through Borovsk and Vereya to Mojaisk,
To recross the battlefield of Borodino:
For this enormous freezing tomb, no obelisk,

But the ground ploughed by cannonballs, harrowed by lances,
Littered with cuirasses, wheels, rags, and thirty thousand
Bodies with no eyes who devoured our glances.

As we passed them, we almost took them for our foes,
And for a moment I thought of dear old Ireland:
Fields of corpses plentiful as dug potatoes.

Spraying the Potatoes

Knapsack-sprayer on my back, I marched the drills
Of blossoming potatoes — Kerr's Pinks in a frivelled blue,
The Arran Banners wearing white. July was due,
A haze of copper sulphate on the far-off hills.

The bronze noon air was drowsy, unguent as glue.
As I bent over the big oil-drum for a refill,
I heard the axle-roll of a rut-locked tumbril.
It might have come from God-knows-where, or out of the blue.

A verdant man was cuffed and shackled to its bed.
Fourteen troopers rode beside, all dressed in red.
It took them a minute to string him up from the oak tree.

I watched him swing in his Derry green for hours and hours,
His popping eyes of apoplectic liberty
That blindly scanned the blue and white potato flowers.

Paddy's Knapsack

One day, raw swedes, potatoes, turnips, barley-seed
And rye — the forage of whatever plundered country —
On another, cheeses, apples, pheasants, jugs of mead,
And honeycombs, blood puddings, fat charcuterie.

Sometimes, the contents of a German butcher's shop,
A Russian prince's cellar, or a Spanish bar;
At times, so much to drink we didn't know when to stop;
At times, so parched we dreamt of water in the jar.

As I open my old knapsack, all comes back to me:
That whiff of Parma ham, gunpowder-tea and snuff,
Aroma of red herrings, phantoms of the liberty

That we enjoyed as fellows of the Harlequin.
I don the mask again, and scent, among the other stuff,
The perfume of a girl whose cloak I pillaged in Turin.

The Ambassadors

Here, let me take you down to the Poppy Fields.
You scent them? They are almost bended for picking.
Here strut the soldiers in their ceremonial shields.
You list them? They are all alive and ticking.

As you can see, the shields are furnished like mirrors
To reflect and shimmer the wavery poppies,
Like bandaged veterans of former bloody wars
For, as you know, all businesses need copies.

I hope I'm not being indiscreet when I reveal
That our President has many body-doubles:
Who knows what is what within the car of armoured steel?

You know, our two states could stand in each other's stead.
Excuse me, Sir, I am sorry for your troubles.
It seems you've got a poppy bullet in your head.

Heart of Oak

Coming to in the Twelfth Meadow, I was still
Woozy with whatever it was had happened me.
I felt like Ahab's Herman Melville,
Regurgitated by a monster of cetacean pedigree.

It'd seemed I'd swum into my own enormous maw
Some months ago. I'd made the rib-cage my abode:
Vaulted hall wherein a swallowed galleon creaked and yawed,
And labyrinths of gloomy light were blue as woad.

In this realm, everything was fitted to my needs:
The Captain's library, his map and compasses,
His davenport, at which I wrote these many screeds,

His microscope, his grand *pianoforte* —
Only the guns and shot were completely useless.
I left them there to rust when I regained my liberty.

Envoy

Now you've travelled through the Land of Nod and Wink,
And sucked the pap of *papaver somniferum*,
In fields abounding in high cockelorum,
You'll find that everything is slightly out of synch.

These words the ink is written in is not indelible
And every fairy story has its variorum;
For there are many shades of pigment in the spectrum,
And the printed news is always unreliable.

Of maidens, soldiers, presidents and plants I've sung;
Of fairies, fishes, horses, and of headless men;
Of beings from the lowest to the highest rung —

With their long ladder propped against the gates of Heaven,
They're queued up to be rewarded for their grand endeavour,
And receive their campaign haloes on the Twelfth of Never.

Acknowledgements

Some of these poems have appeared previously in *Poetry Ireland Review* and the *Irish Review*.

I am grateful to Junko Matoba and her colleagues in the International Association for the Study of Irish Literature, who made it possible for me to visit Tokyo; also Michael and Christine Hinds, who showed me some good bars there. Some of the 'Japanese' poems include versions of, or references to, haiku, particularly those of Bashō. As in *Belfast Confetti* (GalleryBooks, Wake Forest University Press, 1989), these are much indebted to Harold G. Henderson's anthology, *An Introduction to Haiku* (Doubleday Anchor Books, New York, 1958).

Some of the details in the 'Napoleonic' poems have been culled from David G. Chandler's magisterial account, *The Campaigns of Napoleon* (Macmillan Publishing Co., Inc., New York, 1966); also, Philip J. Haythornthwaite, *The Napoleonic Source Book* (Arms and Armour Press, London, 1990), and Philip J. Haythornthwaite and Christopher Warner, *Uniforms of the French Revolutionary Wars* (Arms and Armour Press, 1991). Likewise, I have lifted some details from Laurence Flanagan, *Ireland's Armada Legacy* (Gill & Macmillan, Dublin, 1988).

It would be tedious to give a full account of the folk-song influences on the poems, but Colm O Lochlainn's *Irish Street Ballads* and *More Irish Street Ballads* (Three Candles Ltd., Dublin, 1939 and 1978, published in one volume as *Irish Street Ballads* by Pan Books, London, 1984) were constantly referred to in the writing of this book.

I am grateful to Harry Bradley for pointing out to me that the great Sligo flute player Peter Horan customarily follows the jig 'Wallop the Spot' with another which he calls 'Spot the Wallop'; also to Charlie Piggott, for bringing my attention to *The Blue Shamrock*, an album recorded by Alec Finn.